NOTICE

TO

QUIT

THE GREAT IRISH
FAMINE EVICTIONS

L. PERRY CURTIS, JR.

This essay is part of the interdisciplinary series *Famine Folios*,
covering many aspects of the Great Hunger in Ireland from 1845-52.

CONTENTS

But our whitening bones against ye will rise as witnesses
From the cabins and the ditches, in their charred, uncoffined masses,
For the Angel of the Trumpet will know them as he passes,
A ghastly, spectral army, before the great God we'll stand,
And arraign ye as our murderers, the spoilers of our land.

Speranza (Lady William Wilde), *The Stricken Year* or *The Famine Year* (1847)

VILLAGE OF MOVEEN.

PROLOGUE

The tiny village of Moveen lies in ruins. All but one of the stone cabins is roofless. A wisp of smoke curls upwards from a chimney on the far left. No trees or bushes survive on this barren ground, and no mounds of turf buttress these twenty-odd dwellings. Apart from a solitary man on the right, there are no signs of life. An eerie silence hangs over this once-lively *clachan* in West Clare **[Figure 1]**.[1]

In west Galway the village of Carihaken resembles a graveyard. One man stands forlornly between two empty cabins – the only living creature amidst the skeletal remains of this settlement **[Figure 2]**.

Mienies in County Cork has suffered the same fate. Bereft of life, this desolate scene epitomizes the grim toll taken by starvation and eviction. Similarly the village of Tullig in Kilrush, County Clare has become extinct. Every abode has lost its thatched roof. The only signs of recent habitation are a stack of turf and fragments of furniture. Two burning questions haunt such scenes: where have all the people gone, and why?

These images of destruction and desolation appeared in *The Illustrated London News* (*ILN*) between 1847 and 1850. They were the handiwork of James Mahony, a member of the Cork school of art who had been hired to cover conditions in the west of Ireland during the Great Famine. He also used his pen as the magazine's "special correspondent" to describe what he had witnessed:

Moveen [...] is another ruined village [...][and] a specimen of the dilapidation I behold all around. There is nothing but devastation, while the soil is of the finest description, capable of yielding as much as any land in the empire. Here, at Tullig, and other places, the ruthless destroyer has left the walls of the houses standing, while he has unroofed them and taken away all shelter from the people. They look like the tombs of a departed race, rather than the recent abodes of a yet living people, and I felt actually relieved at seeing one or two half-clad spectres gliding about, as an evidence that I was not in the land of the dead.

Figure 1 | "Village of Moveen" (*ILN*, December 22, 1849)

7

Mahony laid out some depressing statistics: at least 16,000 people had been "unhoused" in the Kilrush Poor Law Union by June 1849; 254,000 holdings between one and five acres had been obliterated between 1841 and 1846; and sixty percent of the poorest tenants had lost their homesteads and livelihoods. As he pointed out with no little irony, all this was done in "the guise of charity and benevolence" (*ILN*, December 22, 1849).

RUINS IN THE VILLAGE OF CARIHAKEN, COUNTY OF GALWAY.

Figure 2 | "Ruins in the Village of Carihaken, County of Galway" (*ILN*, January 5, 1850)

INTRODUCTION

Of all the horrors arising from the successive failures of the potato crop from 1845 to 1852, the most distressing – apart from death caused by disease and starvation – was the loss of hearth and home. No matter how primitive the home – whether a mud-walled hut with a sod roof or a stone-walled cabin with a thatched or slate roof – the violent expulsion of a two - or three-generation family, along with their cherished animals and furnishings, was the cruelest of blows. Equally distressing was the break-up of close family and community ties. One can only imagine the heartbreak of the victims of eviction as they stood outside in the cold and rain watching the bailiffs pull down the roof-beam or set fire to the thatch. Estimates of the numbers evicted between 1849 and 1854 range from half a million to over 700,000 individuals.

Between 1822 and 1845 at least eight partial failures of the "white potato" – otherwise known as "lumpers" and "murphys" – had caused acute hardship. However, the arrival of a hitherto unknown and deadly blight in the autumn of 1845, and the successive crop failures which followed, spelled disaster for almost half of the country's 8.6 million people.

By 1852 more than a million people had died from either famine-related diseases or actual starvation. Overall, death and emigration, both exacerbated by eviction, combined to reduce the population by some 2.5 million between 1841 and 1851.[2]

The loss of the peasant's staple food triggered massive waves of eviction and emigration. Whether the poor surrendered their holdings voluntarily or not, smallholders or cottiers and laborers faced a stark choice between the poorhouse and the nearest port of embarkation. The depopulation of townlands north, west, and south of the River Shannon left behind deserted villages or *clachans* that served as somber reminders of what the agrarian leader Michael Davitt called a "holocaust of humanity" (50).

At the outset of the Famine, a few wealthy landowners tried to stave off starvation by serving soup and bread to destitute families. Thus the Earl of Caledon's agent posted notices around his Tyrone estate announcing the opening of three soup kitchens on

December 28, 1846 for the benefit of "Laborers and Poor Householders."[3] This form of paternalism did not last long in western districts, where the lords of the soil were soon so overwhelmed with beggars that they shut their doors to mendicants.

Thereafter, because so many ardent Christians believed that Divine Providence had delivered this catastrophe to the Irish people as a test of their faith, and because political economists stressed the need to get rid of Ireland's "surplus" populace in order to generate economic growth, few landlords had qualms about purging their estates of profitless peasants. Whether Protestant or Catholic, Irish or Anglo-Irish, the landed elite applied the cold logic of *laissez-faire* to the pauper victims of famine and disease.

In 1845 Elizabeth Smith, a rather "waspish" Anglo-Scottish lady who owned a small estate in county Wicklow, noted in her diary that she had evicted some tenants in order to enlarge their holdings. Having given them some compensation, she described this operation as a "delicate business without annoying anyone." By 1847, however, both the tone and content of her diary had changed: "Alas! the famine progresses, here it is frightful reality to be seen in every face. Idle, improvident, reckless, meanly dependent on the upper classes whom they so abuse [...] here they are starving round us, cold, naked, hungry, well-nigh houseless" (Ó Murchadha, *The Great Famine* 21-2 and 31).[4]

In pre-Famine times the small, scattered settlements along the western seaboard of Munster and Connacht often resounded with music as the inhabitants gathered to share gossip, smoke clay pipes, drink poitín, and dance jigs and reels to a fiddler's lively notes. These mainly Irish-speaking peasants thrived on close ties of kinship and depended on daily social interaction to enrich their otherwise austere lives. The Great Hunger wiped out this communal way of life and scattered the survivors far and wide.

THE CONTEXT OF EVICTION

Three closely intertwined factors account for the impact of the potato blight on the poorest inhabitants of Munster and Connacht. The first was ideological; the second was prejudice – racial and religious; and the third was related to socio-economic structures, including the Poor Law.

The first ideological factor was capitalism, sustained by the principles of political economy known as "the Manchester School" or *laissez-faire*, which championed a free and competitive market unrestricted by tariffs or other government impositions. The free trade lobby justified the huge divisions in social class and wealth by insisting that what was good for the rich was good for the entire nation, because industrious workers or laborers would profit, in the long run, from the concentration of capital in the hands of the few. The pursuit of wealth or capital was seen as a good thing in itself, and did not just benefit plutocrats.

Political economists and their parliamentary allies attributed the stagnation of the Irish economy to the existence of a "redundant" rural population that sapped the country's ability to achieve self-sufficiency. Steeped in the belief that God rewarded hard work as well as devotion, many members of the British governing class looked askance at handouts to the starving hordes in Ireland, whom they considered both lazy and improvident. Charity, they insisted, should be given only to the "deserving poor" or plebeians deemed godly, righteous and sober. Unfortunately for the famine victims, few of them qualified on this score in the eyes of British taxpayers. Consequently, the sooner these profitless peasants disappeared, the better for those left behind. What Ireland sorely needed, it was believed, was a solvent rural bourgeoisie akin to the good old reliable English yeomanry. Echoing the gospel of political economy, the *ILN* criticized the new Irish Poor Law for fostering "idleness and destitution" by diminishing "the natural stimulus to industry" or "exertion," and by "preying on the wealth" still left in the country. In short, it was "only the climax of the ignorant legislation that, operating in silence through ages, has perverted the Irish, and made their naturally fertile abode one scene of desolation" (January 5, 1850). As Peter Gray contends, the interaction of economic and religious imperatives profoundly influenced government responses to the Great Hunger.

As for racial prejudice against the Irish, this sentiment derived from a pervasive belief in a profound cultural, ethnic, and even physiognomic divide between the so-called Anglo-Saxon and Celtic inhabitants of the British Isles [Figure 3]. This conviction had a long history dating back to at least the twelfth century, when Tudor invaders looked down on the native "Irishry" or "Gaels" as barbarians who refused to accept English standards of law and order and dared to resist the expropriation of their land. Sporadic rebellions by the Irish "septs" or clans deepened the mutual antagonism. English courtiers, army officers, and officials condemned the Irish "woodkernes" for resisting their incursion and for resorting to guerrilla warfare, and condoned acts of genocide that drastically reduced the indigenous people. The conquerors insisted on Anglicizing the survivors by whatever means necessary.

Over the centuries this imperial attitude hardened into a form of racial prejudice, supported by new pseudo-sciences that embraced a hierarchical view of the races of man, according to which the Anglo-Saxon and Teutonic races stood at the top of the great racial tree while the Celtic races occupied one of the lower branches. Ardent Anglo-Saxonists were fond of denigrating the Irish peasant – known far and wide as

IRISH PHYSIOGNOMY.

Figure 3 | "Ireland and the Irish: Irish Physiognomy" (*ILN*, October 7, 1843)

"Paddy" – who struck them as epitomizing the vices and weaknesses absent from fully civilized Englishmen. Sooner or later this popular image of witless and feckless Paddy was bound to affect British attitudes towards the use of public funds to relieve the victims of famine across the Irish Sea.

Even before Charles Darwin's *On the Origin of Species* (1859), some British ethnologists and anthropologists detected a physical resemblance between Paddy and the great apes recently discovered in Central Africa. Soon the British reading public embraced the simian origins theory of the Irish race. In his classic text, *The Races of Men: A Fragment* (1850), the influential Scottish anthropologist and anatomist, Robert Knox, declared that Anglo-Saxons were basically "thoughtful, plodding, industrious," in stark contrast to the Celts who were known for their "furious fanaticism; a love of war and disorder; a hatred for order and patient industry." Given their "restless, treacherous [and] uncertain" nature they required "bayonet government." Indeed, they "must be forced from the soil; by fair means if possible, still they must leave," because the purity and integrity of the English race depended on this exodus. The prominent English historian, novelist, and Cambridge lecturer, Charles Kingsley, who extolled Anglo-Saxon virtues, alluded to the hordes of "human chimpanzees" he saw while touring Ireland in 1860. The sight of these semi-simian creatures "along that hundred miles of horrible country" haunted him for months (qtd. in Curtis, *Anglo-Saxons and Celts* 84). The brilliant Scottish essayist and historian, Thomas Carlyle, accused the Irish peasantry with their "wild Milesian features" of having "sunk from decent manhood to squalid apehood" (qtd. in Curtis, *Apes and Angels* 114).[5]

Reinforcing these racist sentiments, London's new comic weekly *Punch* portrayed Paddy as a menacing and semi-simian rebel during the 1840s, when several leading caricaturists began to endow radical Irish nationalists with facial features akin to the chimpanzee. In 1862 Punch published a satirical piece entitled "The Missing Link" that conjured up a tribe of "savages," otherwise known as "the Irish Yahoo," who filled the evolutionary gap between the gorilla and the African Negro. When and if provoked, this hominid was fond of attacking "civilised human beings." However, this violent creature did have one redeeming feature: unlike the gorilla, it could "utter articulate sounds."[6] Whether deadly serious or simply satirical, the appearance of Irish apemen in comic weeklies ranging from London to New York and on to San Francisco during and long after the Famine reflected a powerful undercurrent of Hibernophobia that was bound to harden the attitudes of ethnocentric Englishmen, or Nativist Americans, towards the stereotypical Irishman.

One of *Punch*'s most gifted artists, John Leech, portrayed Paddy as a half-simian peasant with sloping forehead, snub nose, and prognathous or projecting lower jaw akin to the facial features of an ape. Thus in the cartoon "Young Ireland in Business For Himself" (*Punch*, October 18, 1846) he simianized the arms dealer behind the counter while endowing the heavily armed rebel on the right with the tell-tale marks

YOUNG IRELAND IN BUSINESS FOR HIMSELF.

Figure 4 | "Young Ireland in Business For Himself", John Leech (*Punch*, October 18, 1846)

or stigmata of Paddy **[Figure 4]**. Both figures represent not only the physical force wing of Young Ireland but also Paddy's inherently violent and destructive nature.

Leech also drew a brutish and bloated Paddy riding exultingly on the back of a sagging English worker in "The English Labourer's Burden; Or the Irish Old Man of the Mountain" (*Punch*, February 17, 1849) **[Figure 5]**. No doubt this juxtaposition of an honest (and long-suffering) Anglo-Saxon worker and an undeserving Paddy must have pleased members of the English public who resented spending state money on famine relief.

THE ENGLISH LABOURER'S BURDEN;

OR, THE IRISH OLD MAN OF THE MOUNTAIN.

[See *Sinbad the Sailor.*

Figure 5 | "The English Labourer's Burden" (*Punch*, February 17, 1849)

Across the Atlantic the German-born artist Thomas Nast delighted American Nativists a generation later with his savagely satirical images in *Harper's Weekly* of Irish Catholic immigrants invading the shores of America and threatening the Protestant and Yankee establishment. In 1843 J. Kenny Meadows produced his version of simian Paddy dubbed "The Irish Frankenstein" (*Punch*, November 4, 1843). Here the great Catholic nationalist leader, Daniel O'Connell, has conjured up a fiendish monster, namely the campaign to repeal ("REPALE") the Act of Union and create a national assembly in Dublin. Complete with horns and snub nose this menacing creature symbolizes pure evil.

The impact of these satirical images of the Irish on contemporary viewers should not be underestimated. Indeed, the notable absence of protests in England (and America) about such racialized images would suggest that they were relished by all those race-proud Anglo-Saxonists who believed in the greater proximity of Paddy to the anthropoid apes of Africa.

Religious prejudice against the "native Irishry" revolved around the age-old animosity of devout Anglicans and Nonconformists toward the Church of Rome and all its votaries. Most Protestants regarded Roman Catholicism as an idolatrous, if not heathen religion, rooted in superstition and corruption. This anti-Catholic bias had a long and virulent history in England and Scotland where bloodcurdling tales of Catholics massacring Protestants and monks or priests engaging in carnal acts flourished. Evangelicals also accused the Catholic hierarchy of seeking to subvert not only the Established Church but also the equally sacred British constitution. Moreover, the steady flow of poverty-stricken Irish Catholics into British towns generated much hostility against these "alien intruders" whose acceptance of low wages threatened the jobs of British workers – some of whom rioted against Irish railway workers, tunnel diggers, and agricultural laborers for religious, ethnic, and economic reasons.

The dividing line between religious and racial prejudice against Paddy was, of course, blurred. And the resurgence of Roman Catholicism in both countries following O'Connell's successful campaign for Catholic Emancipation and his entry into Parliament in 1829 heaped more fuel on the sectarian fires. Prime Minister Peel's increase of the annual grant to the Catholic seminary at Maynooth in 1845 enraged the anti-Catholic camp, while Pope Pius IX's Rescript in 1859, restoring the Catholic hierarchy in England, created considerable hysteria among Protestants who denounced this so-called "Papal Aggression."[7]

During and after the 1830s a few hardcore English evangelicals became missionaries in western Munster and Connacht hoping to convert the peasantry to the one and only "true faith." Armed with Irish-language Bibles and a little money, they promised local people free housing, food, and education for anyone who sent their children to the new and clean Protestant schools. Catholic priests warned their flocks to avoid these interlopers or "soupers," with their bribes of food and clothing to any Catholic who "turned" (Bowen, *Souperism* passim).[8]

These zealots formed the vanguard of the "Providentialist" school in England that explained the Famine as an act of God designed to test the faith of the Irish people. Adding a note of political economy to this religious equation, Charles Trevelyan, the assistant secretary of the Treasury and chief architect of famine relief policy, declared: "God and nature have imposed [a check] on the too rapid consumption of an insufficient supply" of the staple crop required to feed what he and other policy makers called Ireland's "surplus population." Because the Famine arose out of "God's Providence" it should be allowed to run its course. Combined with the traditional parsimony of the Treasury, such convictions were bound to influence government decisions about relieving the victims of famine and eviction.[9] A leading political economist, Nassau Senior, lamented that the decline in Ireland's "surplus population" would not be large enough to regenerate the economy.[10]

Above and beyond the numerous private charities in the British Isles and America that raised thousands of pounds for relief, many humanitarians as well as dispensary doctors risked their lives by ministering to the victims of dysentery, typhus, and other highly contagious diseases. Among these heroic helpers were Catholic priests, Quakers, and several American evangelicals, too many of whom died from "famine fever."[11]

Figure 6 | **"Young Ireland in Business For Himself"** (*Punch*, October 18, 1846) [Detail of figure 4]

THE POOR LAW

The Irish Poor Law Act of 1838 required landlords to pay a "poor rate" for the support of paupers in the newly built workhouses located in the country's 130 Poor Law Unions. In times of good harvests this safety net sufficed to deal with pauperism. However, the Famine fallout overwhelmed a fragile system that could not hope to cope with all the cottiers and laborers desperate for food and shelter. Because the burden of relief fell heavily on the landlord class they responded, predictably, by evicting paupers in order to avoid paying for their support. Weighed-down with interest payments on huge loans, the landed elite had to choose between purging profitless tenants and plunging into insolvency. Their quandary did not stop British MPs, who lived in comfort far away from the death and disease wracking Ireland, from insisting that Irish property owners should bear the cost of relieving the impoverished masses.

Despite the quadrupling of poor rates since 1846, many Poor Law Unions faced bankruptcy in 1847, by which time thousands of paupers were being denied admission to the already overcrowded workhouses. At the outset of "the Black '47," government food depots and soup kitchens were serving "stirabout" to some three million recipients. However, the mounting cost of this minimal relief soon moved Whig ministers to close the kitchens and curtail outdoor relief. [12]

The workhouses were austere and prison-like institutions where families were broken up and the sexes segregated. Strict regulations governed the inmates, who had to wear coarse uniforms and grind corn or break rocks in order to discourage healthy layabouts from seeking entry. Despite the high risk of contracting fever inside these barracks, countless paupers walked miles to gain entry simply because they wanted to be buried decently and according to the rites of the church, instead of being thrown into unmarked or unconsecrated burial pits. Built to accommodate eight hundred inmates, the Skibbereen workhouse held 1,340 paupers in November 1847; and four years later a thousand were clamoring for admission to the Kilrush workhouse. [13] As for outdoor relief, at the height of the Famine half a million adult males were earning ten pence a day in return for such "task work" as building roads and stone bridges that led nowhere. The thin gruel doled out for this heavy labor failed to relieve the acute pangs of hunger.

Not even the grim conditions inside workhouses came close to matching the horrors outside, where skeletonized beggars thronged rural roads and corpses lay overnight in some towns. As a child the perceptive journalist A. M. Sullivan witnessed "a heap of dead humanity" being carted past the workhouse. At one point he handed a penny to the man bearing a "trap-bottom coffin" designed to dump up to two hundred bodies a day into a "vast charnel pit." Why, he asked in vain, had the English Parliament not intervened "to arrest the hand of brutal landlordism that came to evict the starving tenantry when the sun had set and the moon was in the sky?" (10).

Long before 1845 Irish men, women, and children had emigrated to Britain or elsewhere in search of a better life. Between 1800 and 1845 almost one and a half million people had left the country, largely for economic reasons.[14] After the loss of the potato crop in 1845, however, the exodus became a flood, reaching a peak of 250,000 in 1851. Starved of food and terrified of disease, the peasantry had to choose between quitting their abodes in order to become eligible for indoor relief, and enduring the arduous passage to North America in what were called "coffin ships." Over 2.1 million people, including children, emigrated between 1845 and 1855.[15]

Historians continue to debate the causes of Famine emigration. According to the so-called revisionist or Anglo-centric school, most of those who abandoned their small holdings did so of their own volition, with or without assistance. On the other hand, the anti-revisionists deny that those who left the country did so voluntarily.

Many emigrants quit their homesteads because they knew that by remaining they would starve to death or die of fever. Others were bribed by their landlords to leave with passage money. For example, on his Kerry estate, the 4th Marquis of Lansdowne spent at least £14,000 on passage fees for four thousand of his Glanarought tenants. One third of these people were children and infants. All arrears were forgiven and the pauperized emigrants headed for Liverpool or North America. The vainglorious estate agent, W. Steuart Trench, boasted that this "wholly and entirely voluntary" emigration scheme had saved Lansdowne from bankruptcy while enabling the departing tenants to prosper in the New World. One wonders what would have happened had these families spurned his lordship's offer.[16]

Whether the "pull" factor of gainful employment abroad or the "push" factor of eviction proved stronger remains a moot question.[17] Nevertheless, the surplus mortality rate and the decimation of numerous districts along the west coast cannot be denied. The Whig ministry strove to curtail the cost of relief borne by the Treasury while expecting this purge of unproductive Paddies would go far to jump-start the Irish economy. As the Irish Lord Lieutenant put it, "Priests and patriots howl over the Exodus but the departure of thousands of papist Celts must be a blessing to the country they quit" (Gray 309 and O Cathaoir 166-7). And he was considered one of the more intelligent and moderate Whigs.

EVICTION

For generations after 1850, images of eviction loomed large in the minds of Irish men and women both at home and among the diaspora in "Greater Ireland." Grandparents often told their children's children harrowing tales of the loss of homestead and livelihood. As Woodham-Smith wrote, "fear of eviction was in the very blood of the Irish peasant" long before the arrival of the deadly blight – "and with good reason" (123). This justifiable fear gained huge momentum once mass evictions began in 1846. As late as the mid-twentieth century, the eloquent writer from the Blasket Islands, Maurice O'Sullivan, alluded to these evictions: "Ah, what could the poor people do at that time when the rotten landlords threw out all the tenants at the Cooan and scattered them like little birds?" (52). The collective memory of ejectment and forced emigration haunted Irish communities for generations and gave extra force to the famous battle cry of tenants' rights advocates during the land wars of the 1880s – "The Land for the People."[18]

There was nothing new about evictions in Ireland. During the localized crop failures and famines of 1817, 1822, and 1840, countless tenants had suffered this fate for failure to pay rent. (However, close to half of all notices to quit were not carried out because the insolvent tenant agreed to pay a nominal sum within six months. Failure to meet this obligation was bound to end in dispossession.)[19]

Quite apart from the acute distress of the tenants forced from their homes, some evictors took no pleasure in these operations. Occasionally police constables found eviction duty more distressing than executions, especially when the agent ordered the bailiffs to destroy the dwelling. Most of the decreed tenants left in silence and tears, but some raised their fists and cursed at the sheriff's party. In the words of A. M. Sullivan, who had witnessed such ordeals:

An Irish eviction is a scene to try the sternest nature [...] The anger of the elements affords no warrant for respite or reprieve. In hail or thunder, rain, or snow out the inmate must go. The bed-ridden grandsire, the infant in the cradle, the sick, the aged, and the dying, must alike be thrust forth, though other roof or home the world has naught for them, and the stormy sky must be their canopy during the night at hand (20-21, 252).[20]

Figure 7 | Daniel Macdonald, *Eviction Scene* [Detail]

Indeed, the stormy sky in *Eviction Scene* (c. 1850) (Crawford Art Gallery) **[Figure 7]**, attributed to Daniel Macdonald, augurs ill. The painting shows a farmer reluctantly handing the door key to the agent who is protected by armed soldiers. His wife sobs on his shoulder, and the other women bewail their fate. The grandmother kneels in the traditional pose of supplication. Notwithstanding how well dressed are the victims, the painting insists on their helplessness, while the broken wheel suggests the violent interruption of what had been an enduring cycle of peaceful rural life.

One of the most striking images of eviction dates to a later period. In 1888, while grouse shooting with her husband, Sir William Butler, in Co. Wicklow, Lady Elizabeth Butler heard of an eviction in Glendalough. She rushed to the scene to find the house burnt out, the ground still smoldering, and the bailiffs disappearing from sight. When her subsequent painting of the scene, *Evicted* (1890) (National Folklore Collection, University College Dublin) **[Figure 9]**, was exhibited at the Royal Academy in 1890, the Prime Minister, Lord Salisbury, attempted to soften the ongoing brutality of eviction with an unsavory attempt at humor: "there is such an air of breezy cheerfulness and beauty about the landscape which is painted that it makes me long to take part in an eviction myself," he said (*Times*, May 15, 1890).

Figure 8 | Daniel Macdonald, *Eviction Scene* [Detail of Figure 7]

Figure 9 | Lady Elizabeth Butler, *Evicted*

Roughly akin to "clear cutting" the trees in a forest, the "clearances" on scores of estates left permanent scars on both the landscape and rural society. Defined as the expulsion of more than forty families on the same estate, some 141 clearances took place up to 1853. The landlords involved in this culling of humanity regarded such measures as progress. So too did the prominent Whig, Lord Clarendon, who wanted to "sweep Connaught clean" of 400,000 pauperized peasants because they stood in the way of economic growth **[Figure 10]**.

Much of the rationale for the clearances derived from the passage in 1847 of an amendment to the Irish Poor Law bill, proposed by Sir William Gregory, a Tory landlord from Galway, who insisted on making any tenant holding more than a quarter acre – or one rood – ineligible for indoor relief. In order to enter a workhouse, occupiers above this limit had to surrender their holdings. Many landlords used this clause as a license to evict en masse and then tumble the evictees' cabins to prevent re entry (Donnelly, *CIPF* 116 7).[21] By ousting these smallholders, landlords consolidated the vacant plots into large farms or pasturage to be rented to solvent tenants.

In March 1846 Mrs. Marcella Gerrard, an absentee owner who possessed a small estate in Galway, "rooted out like vermin" in excess of 300 tenants around Ballinlass. According to the *Freeman's Journal*, "they [were] driven from their cabins and their cabins torn down [...] they [were] hunted from these ruins, and the ruins levelled to the earth; seeking refuge in the ditches, they [were] hunted from the ditches." The article went on to lament that the clearance went "without even an echo to answer the stranger when he asks, 'where are they?' Human beings have been used to make way for bullocks!" (March 27, 1846).

News of these evictions infuriated some liberal and radical members of Parliament. Even Lord Londonderry called them "scandalous" and "frightful." Small wonder, he exclaimed, that "assassins walked abroad." In response to a question about her frame of mind following the evictions, Mrs. Gerrard added: "Thank you, I am well, thriving, and getting fat on the curses of the wretches." [22]

SCALP AT CAHUERMORE.

Figure 10 | "Scalp at Cahuermore" (*ILN*, December 29, 1849)

One of the grand masters of clearances was Sir Roger Palmer, who owned 80,000 acres around Ballina, County Mayo. After 1847 his agents forced hundreds of poor families from their homes – often in drenching rain. Every cabin was demolished. A dying man was carried outside only to perish a few hours later. After many of the victims built flimsy lean-tos or "scalpeens" inside their ruined abodes, the "crowbar brigade" returned to tear the walls down and drive them away. An equally avid evictor was the 3rd Earl of Lucan, who turned out 2,000 people and tumbled 300 cottages around Ballinrobe and Castlebar, County Mayo. Some of his house-wreckers worked a six day week and could raze up to twenty houses between dawn and dusk. Lucan then converted most of his 60,000 acres into pasturage leased to graziers. This heavily indebted landlord boasted that he "would not breed paupers to pay priests." Other vigorous evictors in this county included Sir Samuel O'Malley, who uprooted 289 families or 1,441 individuals in 1852, and the 3rd Marquis of Sligo, who had received hardly any rent for three years. Calling the evicted tenants "really idle and dishonest," he took credit for having forgiven the arrears of those who remained. The scale of these clearances earned those responsible the epithet of "exterminators," and any past good deeds they may have performed were quickly forgotten.[23]

The visiting American evangelical, Asenath Nicholson, described the heartrending aftermath of an eviction in 1848 near Newport in County Mayo:

the tumbled cabins, with the poor hapless inmates, who had for years sat around their turf fire, and ate their potatoe together, now lingering and oftimes wailing in despair, their ragged barefoot little ones clinging about them, one on the back of the weeping mother, and the father looking in silent despair, while a part of them are scraping among the rubbish to gather some little relic of mutual attachment [...] then, in a flock, take their solitary, pathless way to seek some rock or ditch, to encamp supperless for the night (Nicholson, *Lights and Shades of Ireland*, qtd. in Gray 73).

This was the inevitable fate of the poor peasants in Erskine Nicol's *An Ejected Family* (1853) (National Gallery of Ireland) **[Figures 11 and 12]**. Nicol's evictees conjure an image of the Holy Family on their flight into Egypt. Known for his condescending, if not downright racialized images, Nicol's invocation of the Holy Family in this painting renders this a more sympathetic image than we usually expect from him.

The clearances around Kilrush in West Clare between November 1847 and June 1850 were devastating. Roughly seventeen percent of the populace lost their homesteads, including a thousand tenants on the estate of Crofton Moore Vandeleur, whose agent, Marcus Keane, earned notoriety for his enthusiastic supervision of evictions that affected some 16,000 persons on the properties under his management. These purges stood out in a county that ranked just below Mayo in the number of expulsions. Keane competed with other agents in the county for the title of most efficient evictor. When summoned to Westminster to defend his actions, he accused

Figure 11 | Erskine Nicol, *An Ejected Family* [Detail of Figure 12]

the evictees of being lazy men of "bad character" or "robbers" whose departure would benefit not just County Clare but the whole country (Ó Murchadha, "The Exterminator General" 176-85 and 187-91). [24]

During 1847-8, Clare landowners obtained over six thousand notices to quit, although roughly half of these were probably not carried out. Nevertheless, the impact of these ejectments could be measured in terms of population loss. Over the course of eighteen months Kilrush union lost 22,000 people and many more left after 1850. In vain a local priest railed against "the murderous proceedings" of the landlord "thugs." While Irish Repealers or nationalists accused the British government of being "a club of gravediggers" and insisted that the country was being "decimated not by the will of God but by the will of Whigs," evictions continued unabated. [25]

Bitter memories of the clearances refused to die. Tangible proof of the "never forgive and never forget" mentality emerged fifty years later when a few men bent on desecration broke into the Keane family vault at Kilmaley, West Clare, and hauled out two heavy lead-lined coffins, burying them nearby. They had no clue as to which one contained Keane's body. Not until 1891 were the purloined coffins discovered, whereupon the evictor's remains were reinterred in the new family mausoleum at Beech Park (Curtis, *DEI* 38-9, 128). [26]

A much smaller and semi-urban clearance took place in May 1849 in the little town of Toomevara near Nenagh, County Tipperary, where some fifty families or five hundred tenants were driven out on the orders of Richard Wilson, the "tyrannical" agent of George Massy Dawson, owner of 19,000 acres. Wilson himself owned most of the town houses on the "hit list" and seemed to take "a devilish delight" in the proceedings. Following these ejectments all the houses were razed. The local workhouse already had over a thousand occupants and could not possibly have accommodated all the evicted families, who sought refuge in "makeshift huts" or scalpeens built nearby. As a local man later recalled, "the only roof for souls was the vault of heaven. Gathering up their fragments of furniture, doors, dressers, old boxes, they built sheds along the channel of the chapel wall and in the school house yard as well as the gardens behind Chapel Street." According to the Tipperary Vindicator, "chairs were arranged in squares, quilts, sheets, and pieces of old canvas were stretched on poles; wigwams were thus formed under whose covering the poor creatures were seated, completely saturated with the rain [...] Asses' cars, and turf baskets were also upturned, and gave shelter to scores of half clad wretches" (O'Brien 35-6). More families were driven out a day or two later. The only protest erupted when the sheriff tried to seize some cattle for unpaid rent. The enraged graziers broke open the gates and released their cattle from the pound. Wilson's operation helped to reduce Toomevara's population by half between 1841 and 1851. These evictions earned him a place in the Irish hall of Famine infamy; and even today mention of his name provokes shudders among residents. [27]

Clearances also took place on the vast Wicklow estate of millionaire absentee landlord the 5th Earl Fitzwilliam of Wentworth Wodehouse in Yorkshire. This Anglo-Irish land and coal magnate had subsidized many emigrants before the Famine. But the pace quickened after 1847 when he culled 850 tenants around Coollattin using both the carrot of passage money and the stick of ejectment decrees. Most of the 4,000 individuals subsidized by this landlord wound up in Canada where they found jobs and saved enough money to send remittances back to relatives to pay for trans-Atlantic passage.[28] Two other proactive emigrators were Sir Robert Gore-Booth and the eminent Whig statesman, Viscount Palmerston, who owned adjacent estates in County Sligo. Both men took pains to oversee the hiring and provisioning of passenger ships to Canada. However, the compensation they offered to tenants upon removal did not spare the former from vilification (James esp. 21-47).

While Lord Palmerston believed that "ejectments ought to be made without cruelty," he contended that Ireland's regeneration depended on "a long, continued and systematic ejectment of Small Holders and of Squatting Cottiers." Only a carefully managed clearance would enable him to square his estate, create ranch farms or increase pasturage – all for the benefit of not just himself, of course, but the country. To achieve this ambitious goal he hired ten vessels in 1847 to transport 2,000 paupers to Canada. On one crowded "coffin ship" almost one third of the passengers died at sea from fever. Another third foundered off the Irish coast, drowning eighty-seven passengers. Those who survived the terrible congestion, disease, foul food, incessant stench, lack of sanitary facilities, and seasickness must have rejoiced, at least initially, when they set foot on land. But on the ships' arrival in Quebec, many local citizens railed against the sickly, unwashed, and half-naked immigrants.[29]

Roughly half of all the evicted dwellings during the Famine era suffered destruction. Whether the thatched roof was set on fire or the roof beams were pulled down, this operation stirred deep anger and dismay among the victims, who stood outside surrounded by their few pieces of furniture, bedding, and utensils. The house-wreckers hired by the agent were usually young men from nearby towns who wielded crowbars, axes, and ropes. Fortified with whiskey or stout, these rough "levellers" or "drivers" had no qualms about destroying the abodes of poor fellow Catholics. Some of them boasted of tumbling as many as ten cabins per day, depending on the distance travelled. Occasionally an agent would pay the evicted tenant up to a pound to level his own cottage while his family stood by sobbing. Seeking to expedite this operation, the notorious landlord, William Scully of Ballycohey, County Tipperary, devised a "machine" made of "massive iron levers, hooks, and chains" that could pull down roof beams when hitched to a horse. The inventor claimed that two such contraptions could wreck ten times as many hovels as fifty crowbar wielders (Curtis, *DEI* 44).

As a child of twelve Sir William Butler, a Catholic who became an able general in the British army, had watched "a crowbar brigade [...] composed of the lowest and most debauched ruffians" razing evicted cottages. Years later he confessed that "if a loaded gun had been put into my hands I would have fired into that crowd of villains, as they plied their horrible trade by the ruined church of Tampul-da-voun" (Butler 11–12).

Figure 12 | Erskine Nicol, *An Ejected Family*

GRAPHIC IMAGES OF EVICTION

Why were there so few depictions of the toll taken by the Famine? Irish artists with ambition gravitated towards the market in London, where wealthy patrons did not want to be confronted with unacceptable subject matter of oppression, distress, or starvation – especially from the hands of an Irish artist.[30] Paradoxically, a number of English artists did depict social conditions in Ireland. Frederick Goodall, Francis Topham and Alfred Fripp made a number of visits to the West in the 1840s, but their homely scenes of domesticity were rendered harmless by sentimentalization. Goodall's *An Irish Eviction* (1850) (New Walk Museum and Gallery, Leicester) is a rare and rather clunky attempt at representing the vile practice.

George Frederic Watts's *The Irish Famine* (c.1848–1850) (The Watts Gallery, Guildford) **[Figure 13]**, showing a huddled family dominating a barren landscape, is a more commanding image, but it was a work of the imagination. Watts only visited Ireland after he painted this picture. On the one hand, the anatomical fullness of the figures shows just how little Watts knew of famine; on the other, he demonstrates his interest in not offending the sensibilities of English audiences, instead confirming the views of many: here go the Irish, fit and healthy, looking for undeserved English charity.

By way of contrast, the impact of Robert George Kelly's retaliatory picture, *An Ejectment in Ireland (A Tear and a Prayer for Erin)* (1848, reworked and retitled 1851) (private collection) **[Figure 14]** was neutralized by contemporary reviews that described the painting as "vulgarly treated" and artistically inferior (*ILN*, February 26, 1853). The handsome tenant stands tall, with cudgel in hand as he struggles against his arrest for having assassinated a bailiff. In vain his little son tries to push one constable away. His wife and mother kneel in supplication as the priest raises his arm toward heaven while consoling the woman who cradles her infant. Inevitably, in the distance we see the sheriff's party and cavalrymen march down the winding road toward the next eviction site.

Figure 13 | Frederic Watts, *The Irish Famine*

Figure 14 | Robert George Kelly, *An Ejectment in Ireland (A Tear and a Prayer for Erin)*

More surprisingly, given the newness of the medium and the somewhat more heterogeneous audiences, few pictorial newspapers captured the physical act of evictions in progress. A notable exception was Edmund Fitzpatrick's *Ejectment of Irish Tenantry* (*ILN*, December 16, 1848) **[Figure 15]**, wherein bailiffs are busy carrying out the worldly goods of a peasant family from their wretched hovel, stripping the sod roof, and distraining chattel, while the tenant and his wife plead in vain for a reprieve.

Like their painter colleagues, illustrators tended to avoid sketching half-naked, emaciated or dying beggars, thereby "sanitizing" the human fallout from the Famine.[31] But James Mahony was an exception. His sketches of "misery and mortality" featured mothers desperately seeking food and shelter for their dying children, thereby making women the iconic victims of the Famine. Although the *ILN* did express sympathy for the victims of hunger and disease, it blamed the clearances on the new Poor Law and the rise in the Poor Law rates that gave landlords "no choice" but to evict. As one editor put it:

these evictions [...] are not merely a legal but a natural process; and however much we may deplore the misery from which they spring, and which they so dreadfully aggravate, we cannot compel the Irish proprietors to continue in their miserable holdings the wretched swarms of people who pay no rent, and who prevent the improvement of the property so long as they remain upon it (*ILN*, October 20, 1849).

No friend of the landlords, whom he accused of selfishness and "extirpating the people instead of aiding and encouraging their exertions," Mahony echoed some political economists by denouncing the Irish Poor Law because it promoted "idleness and destitution" and thereby diminished "the natural stimulus to industry, which decreases wealth" (*ILN*, January 5, 1850 and February 9, 1850).

During the late 1840s the words "eviction" and "extermination" became synonymous. One remarkable feature of evictions, however, was the absence of organized resistance. Unlike the land wars towards the end of the century, when countless tenants fortified their cabins and fought pitched battles against the evictors, few famine-stricken smallholders defended their homesteads. Apart from some raised fists and curses, the majority meekly accepted their fate, if only because they were too demoralized, debilitated, and unorganized to resist.

Most of the British national and provincial press accorded the clearances only sporadic coverage with the result that the evictors were spared a good deal of abuse. Editors and reporters in the mainstream press justified the evictions as necessary for the social and economic improvement of the country.

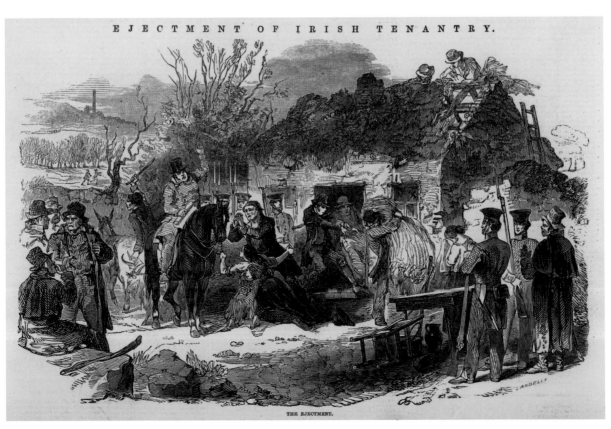

EJECTMENT OF IRISH TENANTRY.

THE EJECTMENT.

Figure 15 | "Ejectment of Irish Tenantry", Edmund Fitzpatrick (*ILN*, December 16, 1848)

EPILOGUE

Between 1845 and 1854, close to half a million men, women, and children suffered eviction. At least 200,000 of these were driven out between 1845 and 1849 when the Royal Irish Constabulary began counting. According to Dublin Castle, 66,469 families suffered "actual evictions" between 1846 and 1852, for a total of 332,345 persons. [32]

Of course it is far easier to play with numbers than to comprehend their significance. This seismic uprooting of people, and the attendant rise in mortality, underscore the utter failure of the Act of Union or the British government to cope with Ireland's ordeal.

While the Great Hunger reduced the population by almost one quarter within a decade and put an end to the "rundale" system of land occupation and reckless subdivision, it also produced the major shift away from tillage and towards pasturage, often known as "the shift from corn to horn," along with the commercialization of agriculture west of the River Shannon. Apart from the victims of famine and eviction, the losers were insolvent landlords. And the winners were wealthier landlords and investors from northeast Ulster and Britain who bought estates in the Encumbered Estates Court, along with the strong farmers and graziers who formed an assertive rural bourgeoisie that would dominate Irish politics in the place of the old landed elite.

Words and pictures can never do justice to the trauma of eviction – even if many of the dispossessed did find a better life in the New World. In his address to the synod at Thurles in 1850, Cardinal Paul Cullen declared that:

the desolating track of the exterminator is to be traced in too many parts of the country – in those levelled cottages and roofless abodes where so many virtuous and industrious families have been torn by brute force, without distinction of age or sex, sickness or health, and flung upon the highway to perish in the extremity of want (qtd. in O' Cathaoir 168).

The land system, the landlord class, the ideology of *laissez-faire* and the relentless pursuit of profit, the lethal force of Mother Nature, and British government policy all bear some responsibility for the catastrophic consequences of *An Gorta Mór*. While the refusal of Whig ministers to spend more than £7 million on famine relief, and their insistence that Irish property should pay for Irish poverty, greatly aggravated the disaster, they did not deliberately conspire to reduce Ireland's "surplus" population by almost one third – however much the political economists welcomed this loss.

ENDNOTES

[1] Kevin Whelan defines a *clachan* as a *baile* or "a nucleated group of farmhouses, where land-holding was organized communally [...] and often with considerable ties of kinship between the families involved" (esp. 23–24).

[2] Chief among the standard works on the Famine are Woodham-Smith; Edwards and Williams; Bourke; Ó Gráda, *The Great Irish Famine* (hereafter *GIF*), *Black '47*, and *Ireland: A New Economic History* 173-91; Donnelly, *The Great Irish Potato Famine* (hereafter, *GIPF*); Ó Murchadha, *The Great Famine* (hereafter *GF*); Kinealy, *This Great Calamity* (hereafter *GC*); Gray; Nally; and Crowley, Smyth, and Murphy.

[3] Signed by the agent Henry L. Prentice, this printed "NOTICE" also addressed a message to the children of laborers, seeking to "encourage useful industry." Thus he wrote: "I hereby offer a Premium of 2d. per Bushel, for Bruised or Pounded Whin/gorse or furze/Tops, properly prepared as for Horses and Cows." The agent expected tenants to support this "useful occupation" because feeding cattle required "the strictest economy." Curtis MSS.

[4] See also Thomson xviii and 113.

[5] For the many aspersions cast on the Irish or Celtic race in Victorian England, see Curtis, *Anglo-Saxons and Celts* and *Apes and Angels*; de Nie; N. O'Sullivan *Aloysius O'Kelly* and "The Tombs;" Gibbons; McBride.

The sundry critics of the "simianizing of Paddy thesis" include first and foremost Foster, *Paddy and Mr. Punch*, followed by Gilley, and Moran.

For an exhaustive structural analysis of Mr. Punch's stereotyping of Paddy, see Weimer.

[6] See also Curtis, *Apes and Angels* 100.

[7] For popular Protestantism in England and the backlash of the Ecclesiastical Titles Act (1851), see Norman 23-79; Bowen, *The Protestant Crusade* 229-33; Hoppen 145-6, 443; and Best. For hostility to Irish workers in Britain, see Redford 150-64.

[8] See also Bowen, *The Protestant Crusade* 185-9, 223-4, 241-2 and 251-2, and I. Whelan.

[9] The English historian Geoffrey Best wondered: "Is the large extent of English indifference to the Irish Famine partly explicable in terms of a protestant acquiescence in divine Justice? Did a double-barreled hostility to the Irish and to Popery anywhere else remain as big a part of popular toryism as it seems to have done in Liverpool?" (Best 142).

[10] Gray esp. 24-6, 120-1, 135-7, and 228-57; Kinealy, *GC* esp. 111-2, 118-9,137-8, 156-7, 179-80, 248-9, and 349-55.

[11] For the heroic efforts of famine relief workers, *see inter* alia Woodham-Smith 156-74; Donnelly, *GIPF* 79-82; Ó Murchadha, *GF* 83-98; and Kinealy *GC* esp. 147-67 and 237.

[12] Donnelly, *GIPF* 81-92; Kinealy *GC* 90-157; *The Illustrated London News*, January 5, 1850. By 1849, forty-three percent of County Clare's population was receiving relief.

[13] *Cork Examiner*, November 1, 1847; O'Cathaoir 168. The rigors of the Irish poor law and workhouse system are discussed in Donnelly, *GIPF* 2-3, 92, 96-7, and 101-19; Kinealy, *GC* 106-16 and "The Role of the Poor Law during the Famine;" Ó Murchadha, *GF* 75-6, 95-111, 129, 139-40, 164, 167; and Smyth, "The Creation of the Workhouse System" and "Classify, Confine, Discipline."

[14] For the exodus or "pilgrimage" out of Ireland, see Woodham-Smith 270-6; MacDonagh, "Irish Overseas Emigration" 319-88; Donnelly, *GIPF* 94, 179-80; Fitzpatrick 175-84; Gray 97-115; and Kinealy, *GC* 297-401.

[15] For cogent accounts of the mass exodus after 1846, see MacDonagh, "Irish Emigration to the United States;" Kinealy, *GC* 297-341; Ó Gráda, *Black '47*, 104-21; and Miller.

[16] Lyne xvii-xxx, l-lvi, 39-68, and 195-201; Curtis, *Depiction of Eviction* 52; Kinealy, *GC* 312-3.

[17] For revisionist interpretations, see Foster, *Modern Ireland* 318-37; Daly; Boyce 170; Norton esp. 292-302; and Paseta 38-9.

For a classic example of Irish-American anti-revisionism, see Gallagher.

Further discussion about the historiographical debate over the Great Famine may be found in Gray 178-83.

[18] Edna O'Brien alludes to the psychological burden of eviction in her fictionalized memoir, *Saints and Sinners*. Her grandmother told her about how "our forebears" had been "driven from their holdings and their cabins down the years. She said that the knowledge of eviction and the fear of the poorhouse were in our blood" (185).

[19] Vaughan 29-34.

[20] For Sullivan's vivid account of famine horrors, see also "The Black Forty-Seven," *New Ireland 57-68.*

[21] See also Donnelly, "Mass Eviction;" Ó Murchadha, *GF* 100, 116-7; and 192; and Kinealy *GC* 23, 181, and 216-27.

[22] The Ballinlass evictions gave rise to the phrase "to Gerrardise," meaning to evict in a "vindictive" manner (Curtis, *DEI* 36-7).

[23] Ó Murchadha, *GF* 113-28; Kinealy, *GC* 116, 224; Donnelly "Mass Evictions" 155-9 and *GIPF* 158; Curtis, *DEI* 36-8; and Jordan 67-70 and 111-6.

[24] See also Ó Murchadha, *GF* 131-2; Donnelly, *GIPF* 144-56; Curtis, *DEI* 38-9.

[25] Donnelly, "Mass Eviction" 162-73; Vaughan 25-7; and Ó Murchadha, *GF* 122-25.

[26] See also Ó Murchadha, "The Exterminator General".

[27] One Toomevara resident named his crippled dog Wilson and whenever he saw the agent, he would shout: "Wilson little dog, you cripple, come on" (qtd. in H. O'Brien 44-6, 48-9).

[28] Donnelly, *TGIPF* 178-86; Ó Murchadha, *GF* 140-9; Kinealy, *GC* 101-2, 297-339.

[29] Gray 192; Woodham-Smith 204-69; MacDonagh, *A Pattern* 29-31, 48-51; Curtis, *DEI* 52, 333; and Ó Murchadha, *GF* 140. For the appalling conditions on board these "coffin ships," see Gallagher 179-233.

[30] For further discussion on artistic practices and conventions during the Famine period, see N. O'Sullivan, "Lines of Sorrow."

[31] See Crawford 76 and 84, as well as Kissane 50.

[32] Vaughan 23-6 and 230; Donnelly, *GIF* 139-40 and "Mass Evictions" 155; Ó Gráda, *Black '47* 44. According to Kinealy, 65,515 families or approximately 327,575 persons were evicted between 1847 and 1851 – amounting to "more than 2.5 percent of all agricultural holders" (*GC* 218). One of the highest estimates – 190,00 families in three years (1849-51) – appeared in Michael Mulhall's popular *Dictionary of Statistics* (175) – a figure endorsed by Davitt in his *Fall of Feudalism* (68). Tim P. O'Neill provides a more credible upper limit of 724,000 persons evicted between 1849 and 1854 (39-48).

WORKS CITED

A Guide to Ireland's Great Hunger Museum: Músaem An Ghorta Mhóir. Hamden, CT.: Quinnipiac UP / Ireland's Great Hunger Museum, 2012.

Best, G. F. A. "Popular Protestantism in Victorian Britain." *Ideas and Institutions of Victorian Britain*. Ed. Robert Robson. London: G. Bell and Sons, 1967. 115–142.

Bourke, Austin. *The Visitation of God?: The potato and the great Irish famine*. Eds. Jacqueline Hill and Cormac Ó Gráda. Dublin: Lilliput Press, 1993.

Bowen, Desmond. *Souperism: Myth or Reality? A Study in Souperism*. Cork: Mercier, 1971.

---. *The Protestant Crusade in Ireland, 1800-70: A Study of Protestant-Catholic Relations Between the Act of Union and Disestablishment*. Dublin: Gill and Macmillan, 1978.

Boyce, David George. *Nationalism in Ireland*. 2nd ed. London: Routledge, 1991.

Butler, William Francis, and Eileen Butler. *Sir William Butler, an Autobiography*. London: Constable, 1911.

Crawford, Margaret. "The Great Irish Famine 1845-9: image versus reality." *Ireland: Art into History*. Eds. Raymond Gillespie and Brian P. Kennedy. Dublin: Town House, 1994. 75-90.

Crowley, John, William J. Smyth, and Mike Murphy, eds. *Atlas of the Great Irish Famine*. Cork: Cork UP, 2012.

Cullen, Fintan. *The Irish Face: Redefining the Irish Portrait*. London: National Portrait Gallery, 2004.

Curtis, L. Perry. *Anglo-Saxons and Celts: A Study of Anti-Irish Prejudice in Victorian England*. Bridgeport, Conn.: Published by the Conference on British Studies at the University of Bridgeport; [distributed by New York UP, New York], 1968.

---. *Apes and Angels: The Irishman in Victorian Caricature*. Washington D.C.: Smithsonian Institution, 1971.

---. *Depiction of Eviction in Ireland: 1845-1910*. Dublin: University College Dublin, 2011.

Daly, Mary E. *The Famine in Ireland*. Dublin: Published for the Dublin Historical Association by Dundalgan Press, 1986.

Davitt, Michael. *The Fall of Feudalism in Ireland*. London: Harper & Bros., 1904.

de Nie, Michael Willem. *The Eternal Paddy: Irish Identity and the British Press, 1798-1882*. Madison: University of Wisconsin, 2004.

Donnelly, James S. *The Great Irish Potato Famine*. Gloucestershire: Sutton, 2001.

---. "Mass Eviction and the Great Famine: The Clearances Revisited." *The Great Irish Famine*. Ed. Cathal Póirtéir. Dublin: Mercier, 1995. 155-173.

Dufferin, Lord, and G. F. Boyle. *Narrative of a Journey from Oxford to Skibbereen during the Year of the Irish Famine*. 3rd ed. Oxford: John Henry Parker, 1847.

Edwards, R. Dudley, and T. Desmond Williams, eds. *The Great Famine: Studies in Irish History, 1845-52*. New York: New York UP, 1957.

Fitzpatrick, David. "Flight from Famine." *The Great Irish Famine*. Ed. Cathal Póirtéir. Dublin: Mercier, 1995. 175-84.

Foster, R. F. *Modern Ireland, 1600-1972*. London: Allen Lane, 1988.

---. *Paddy and Mr Punch: Connections in Irish and English History* London: Penguin, 1995.

Gallagher, Thomas Michael. *Paddy's Lament: Ireland 1846-1847*. New York: Harcourt Brace Jovanovich, 1982.

Gibbons, Luke. *Limits of the Visible: Representing the Great Hunger*. Hamden, CT: Quinnipiac UP / Ireland's Great Hunger Museum, 2014.

---. "Race against Time: Racial Discord and Irish History." *Transformations in Irish Culture*. Luke Gibbons. Cork: Cork UP, 1996. 149-63.

Gilley, Sheridan. "English Attitudes to the Irish in England, 1780-1900." *Immigrants and Minorities in British Society*. Ed. Colin Holmes. London: Allen and Unwin, 1978. 81-110.

Gray, Peter. *Famine, Land, and Politics: British Government and Irish Society, 1843-1850*. Dublin: Irish Academic Press, 1999.

Hoppen, K. Theodore. *The Mid-Victorian Generation, 1846-1886*. Oxford: Clarendon Press, 1998.

James, Dermot. *The Gore-Booths of Lissadell*. Dublin: Woodfield, 2004.

Jordan, Donald. *Land and Popular Politics in Ireland*. Cambridge: Cambridge UP, 1994.

Kinealy, Christine. *This Great Calamity: The Irish Famine, 1845-52*. Dublin: Gill & Macmillan, 1994.

---. "The Role of the Poor Law during the Famine." *The Great Irish Famine*. Ed. Cathal Póirtéir. Dublin: Mercier, 1995. 104-22.

Kissane, Noel. *The Irish Famine: A Documentary History*. Dublin: National Library of Ireland, 1995.

Knox, Robert. *The Races of Men: A Fragment*. Philadelphia: Lea & Blanchard, 1850.

Lyne, Gerard J. *The Lansdowne Estate in Kerry under the Agency of William Steuart Trench, 1849-72*. Dublin: Geography Publications, 2001.

MacDonagh, Oliver. "Irish Overseas Emigration during the Famine." *The Great Famine*. Eds. R. Dudley Edwards and T. Desmond Williams. New York: New York UP, 1957.

---. "Irish Emigration to the United States of America and the British Colonies During the Famine." *The Great Famine*. Eds. R. Dudley Edwards and T. Desmond Williams. New York: New York UP, 1957. 317-88.

---. *A Pattern of Government Growth, 1800-60: The Passenger Acts and Their Enforcement*. London: MacGibbon & Kee, 1961.

McBride, Lawrence, "Historical Imagery in Irish Political Illustration 1880-1910," *New Hibernia Review* 2.3 (Spring 1998): 9-25.

Miller, Kerby A. "Emigration to North America in the era of the Great Famine, 1845-55." *Atlas of the Great Irish Famine*. Eds. John Crowley, William J. Smyth, Mike Murphy. Cork: Cork UP, 2012. 214-227.

Moran, Gerard. "The Imagery of the Irish Land War, 1880-1890." *Images, Icons and the Irish Nationalist Imagination*. Ed. Lawrence W. McBride. Dublin: Four Courts, 1999. 37-52.

Mulhall, Michael George. *The Dictionary of Statistics*. London: Ballantyne, 1884.

Nally, David P. *Human Encumbrances: Political Violence and the Great Irish Famine*. Indiana: Notre Dame, 2011.

Nicholson, Asenath. *Lights and Shades of Ireland*. London: William Tweedie, 1850.

Norman, E. R. *Anti-Catholicism in Victorian England*. New York: Barnes and Noble, 1968.

Norton, Desmond. *Landlords, Tenants, Famine: The Business of an Irish Land Agency in the 1840s*. Dublin: University College Dublin, 2006.

O'Brien, Edna. *Saints and Sinners*. London: Faber and Faber, 2011.

O'Brien, Helen. *The Famine Clearance in Toomevara, County Tipperary*. Dublin: Four Courts, 2010.

Ó Cathaoir, Brendan. *Famine Diary*. Dublin: Irish Academic Press, 1999.

Ó Gráda, Cormac. *Black '47 and Beyond: The Great Irish Famine in History, Economy, and Memory*. Princeton, N.J.: Princeton UP, 1999.

---. *The Great Irish Famine*. Dublin: Macmillan, 1989.

---. *Famine: A Short History*. Princeton, N.J.: Princeton UP, 2009.

---. *Ireland: A New Economic History*, 1780-1939. Oxford: Clarendon, 1994.

Ó Murchadha, Ciarán. "The Exterminator General of Clare: Marcus Keane of Beech Park." *County Clare Studies: Essays in Memory of Gerald O'Connellm, Sean O Murchadha, Thomas Coffey and Pat Flynn*. Ed. Ciarán Ó Murchadha. Ennis: Clare Archaeological and Historical Society, 2000.

---. *The Great Famine: Ireland's Agony 1845-1852*. London: Continuum International Group, 2011.

O'Neill, Tim P. "Famine Evictions." *Famine, Land and Culture in Ireland*. Ed. Carla King. Dublin: University College Dublin Press, 2000. 29-58.

O'Sullivan, Maurice. *Twenty Years A-Growing*. New York: Viking, 1933.

O'Sullivan, Niamh. *Aloysius O'Kelly: Art, Nation, Empire*. Dublin: Field Day Publications, 2010.

---. *The Tombs of a Departed Race: Illustrations of Ireland's Great Hunger*. Hamden, CT: Quinnipiac UP / Ireland's Great Hunger Museum, 2014.

---. "Lines of Sorrow: Representing Ireland's Great Hunger." *Ireland's Great Hunger Museum Inaugural Catalogue*. (Hamden, CT: Quinnipiac UP, 2012).

Paseta, Senia. *Modern Ireland: A Very Short Introduction*. Oxford: Oxford UP, 2003.

Póirtéir, Cathal, ed. *The Great Irish Famine*. Dublin: Mercier, 1995.

Redford, Arthur. *Labour Migration in England, 1800-1850*. Ed. W.H. Chalouer. File Copy ed. Manchester: Manchester UP, 1976.

Smyth, William J. "Classify, confine, discipline and punish – the Roscrea Union: A microgeography of the workhouse system during the Famine." *Atlas of the Great Irish Famine*. Eds. John Crowley, William J. Smyth, Mike Murphy. Cork: Cork UP, 2012. 128-144.

---. "The Creation of the Workhouse System." *Atlas of the Great Irish Famine*. Eds. John Crowley, William J. Smyth, Mike Murphy. Cork: Cork UP, 2012. 120-127.

Sullivan, A. M. *New Ireland*. Philadelphia: J.B. Lippincott, 1878.

Thomson, David, ed. *The Irish Journals of Elizabeth Smith, 1840-50*. Oxford: Clarendon, 1980.

Vaughan, W. E. *Landlords and Tenants in Mid-Victorian Ireland*. Oxford: Clarendon, 1994.

Whelan, Irene. *The Bible War in Ireland: The "Second Reformation" and the Polarization of Protestant-Catholic Relations, 1800-1840*. Madison, Wis.: University of Wisconsin, 2005.

Whelan, Kevin. "Pre and Post-Famine Landscape Change." *The Great Irish Famine*. Ed. Cathal Póirtéir. Dublin: Mercier, 1995.

Weimer, Martin. *Das Bild Der Iren Und Irlands Im Punch, 1841-1921*. Mainz: P. Lang, 1993.

Woodham-Smith, Cecil. *The Great Hunger*. London: H. Hamilton, 1962.

IMAGES

Cover

Alexander Williams, RHA
1846-1930
Cottage, Achill Island
Oil on canvas
24 x 42 in (61 x 106.7 cm)
© Ireland's Great Hunger Museum

Figure 1

"Village of Moveen"
The Illustrated London News
December 22, 1849

Figure 2

"Ruins in the Village of Carihaken,
County of Galway"
The Illustrated London News
January 5, 1850

Figure 3

"Ireland and the Irish: Irish Physiognomy"
The Illustrated London News
October 7, 1843

Figure 4

John Leech
"Young Ireland in Business for Himself"
Punch
October 18, 1846

Figure 5

John Leech
"The English Labourer's Burden"
Punch
February 17, 1849

Figure 6

Detail of Figure 4

Figure 7

Daniel Macdonald
1821-1853
Eviction Scene
c. 1850
Oil on canvas
24.8 x 29.5 in (63 x 75 cm)
Crawford Art Gallery, Cork

Figure 8

Detail of Figure 7

Figure 9

Lady Elizabeth Butler
1846-1933
Evicted
1890
Oil on canvas
51.6 x 76.3 in (131 x 194 cm)
National Folklore Collection,
University College Dublin

Figure 10

"Scalp at Cahuermore"
The Illustrated London News
December 29, 1849

Figure 11

Detail of Figure 12

Figure 12

Erskine Nicol
1825-1904
An Ejected Family
1853
Oil on canvas
19.7 x 32.3 in (50 x 82 cm)
Photo © National Gallery of Ireland
NGI.4577

Figure 13

George Frederic Watts
1817-1904
The Irish Famine
1850
Oil on canvas
71 x 77.95 in (180.3 x 198 cm)
Watts Gallery, Compton, Surrey, UK
©Trustees of Watts Gallery
Bridgeman Images

Figure 14

Robert George Kelly
*An Ejectment in Ireland
(A Tear and a Prayer for Erin)*
1848-51
Owned by Anthony John Mourek
Image provided by Irish Arts Review

Figure 15

Edmund Fitzpatrick
"Ejectment of Irish Tenantry"
The Illustrated London News
December 16, 1848

Images provided by Ireland's Great Hunger Museum,
Quinnipiac University unless otherwise noted.

L. PERRY CURTIS, JR.

.

ABOUT THE AUTHOR

L. Perry Curtis, Jr. is professor emeritus of history at Brown University. His forty-year teaching career also included appointments at Princeton University and The University of California, Berkeley. Educated at Yale and Oxford, he specialized in modern British and Irish history with an emphasis on Anglo-Irish political and cultural relations. His publications include: *Apes and Angels: The Irishman in Victorian Caricature* (1971, rev. ed. 1997), *Jack the Ripper and the London Press* (2001), and *The Depiction of Eviction in Ireland, 1845-1910* (2011).

IRELAND'S GREAT HUNGER MUSEUM | QUINNIPIAC UNIVERSITY PRESS ©2015

SERIES EDITORS

Niamh O'Sullivan
Grace Brady

IMAGE RESEARCH

Claire Puzarne

DESIGN

Rachel Foley

ACKNOWLEDGMENT

Office of Public Affairs, Quinnipiac University

PUBLISHER

Quinnipiac University Press

PRINTING

GRAPHYCEMS

ISBN 978-0-9904686-6-0

Ireland's Great Hunger Museum
Quinnipiac University

3011 Whitney Avenue
Hamden, CT 06518-1908
203-582-6500

www.ighm.org